Read Along Rhymes

These rhyming stories help to make early reading an exciting, enjoyable shared experience for children, parents and teachers. They are designed to be read by adult and child together, or by children in pairs. The 'join-in' or 'read along' text is contained in speech bubbles, giving children an active role in the story-telling. The pictures and speech bubbles together give the outline of the story – the full story is told in the verse below. *Read Along Rhymes* can be used in conjunction with any reading programme.

The stories can be used flexibly, as perfect 'take-home books', linking home and school. They can also be used by teachers as part of their language programme, matching a book to a child, and developing the content within each book.

Read Along Stories

If you've enjoyed *Read Along Rhymes* you will be sure to get a lot of fun out of *Read Along Stories* (25 titles).

1	The Hungry Snake	14	The Little Indian
2	Fresh Fish on Friday	15	The Strange Umbrella
3	The Mischievous Monkey	16	The Envious Elephant
4	Gilbert the Goat	17	An Orange for the Baby
5	Hen Looks for a House	18	The Magic Vase
6	The Clever Worm	19	The Two Wizards
7	The Robber Rat	20	The King who Couldn't Kick
8	Dirty Dan	21	The Queen who Wouldn't be Quiet
9	Mr Tubb's Tap	22	Snakes and Ladders
10	The Witch's Ball	23	Yawn Yawn Yawn
11	Ant's Apple	24	A Jumper for Grumper
12	Nails for Newt	25	Peter's Pink Panda
13	Cat's Cake		

Suggestions to parents

It's a good idea to try and find a quiet place to sit together, away from distractions. First look through the pictures together, stop and talk about what's happening in the story: what's in the pictures, how the characters are feeling, what's going to happen next, and so on. You can have fun with the repetitions, the exclamations and the rollicking rhythms of the verse.

Dreadful Dragons

There once were two dragons called Dodo and Dot
Who didn't like fighting and killing a lot.
'We're not dreadful dragons, we don't like to fight.
We're happier dusting than chasing a knight.'

'We'd rather grow daisies and bright daffodils
Than breathe fire for the knights to practise their skills.
We've just started digging or picking our flowers
When a knight gallops up – wants to try out his powers.'

'Or sometimes we're cooking some dumplings and stew,
When a knight rides up shouting, 'Please fight me, you two!'
Or we're making some doughnuts, just squirting the jam,
When a knight dashes in and bashes us WHAM!'

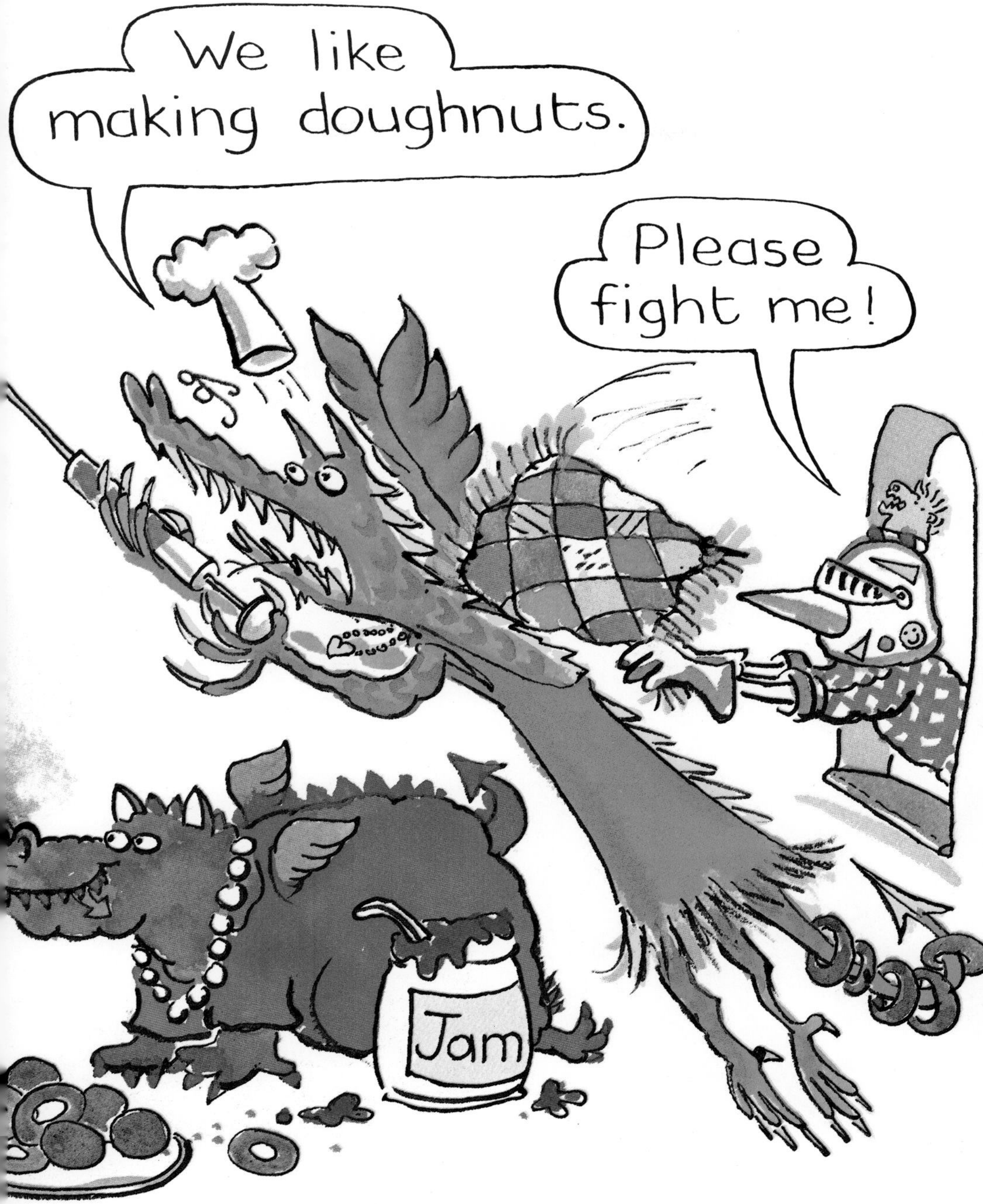
We like making doughnuts.
Please fight me!
Jam

Sometimes we're throwing our darts at the board,
When a knight swipes them off with the tip of his sword.
Or maybe we're drawing or playing the drum,
When a knight charges up and spoils all the fun.'

'Then we have to stop playing, pretend to give chase
And start breathing fire all over the place.
We're tired of this fighting, it makes such a mess.
There's a burn in the door and a hole in Dot's dress.'

'The deckchair's in pieces, the dustbin's upturned,
The daisies are scorched, the doughnuts are burned.
It *is* such a nuisance, there *must* be a way
To keep off these knights, so they'll leave us to play.'

'Let's dig a deep ditch which goes all the way round.
We'll fill it with water and the knights will get drowned!'
So the two started digging, it took them a week.
They dug till they dropped, too worn out to speak.

They next built a drawbridge which could be let down,
Whenever they wanted to go into town.
They drove down the road in an open-air truck
And everyone waved and wished them good luck.

They built a new house in a month and a day
With two dozen rooms and a barn full of hay.
And when in the winter the ditch filled with rain,
Those knights didn't bother the dragons again.

The first of the knights who dared it and tried
Spent the rest of the day being wrung out and dried.
The next of the knights who decided to dive
Nearly froze with the cold and *just* came out alive!

Now Dodo and Dot are as happy can be.
They sit in their deckchairs drinking dandelion tea.
They feed their new ducks and make daisy chains.
They dig in the garden and swim when it rains.

'We're not dreadful dragons, we don't like to fight.
We're happier dusting than chasing a knight.'

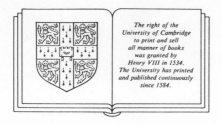

The right of the
University of Cambridge
to print and sell
all manner of books
was granted by
Henry VIII in 1534.
The University has printed
and published continuously
since 1584.

Published by the Press Syndicate of the University of Cambridge
The Pitt Building, Trumpington Street, Cambridge CB2 1RP
32 East 57th Street, New York, NY 10022, USA
10 Stamford Road, Oakleigh, Melbourne 3166, Australia

© Cambridge University Press 1989

First Published 1989

Printed in Hong Kong by Wing King Tong

British Library cataloguing in publication data
Potter, Tessa
  Dreadful dragons
    1. English language. Readers – For children
    I. Title II. Vyvyan-Jones, Marc III. Series
    428.6

ISBN 0 521 35491 9 hard covers
ISBN 0 521 35756 X paperback

DS